American History & Government

Four Battles of the Civil War

by
Carrie Hall

Don Johnston Incorporated
Volo, Illinois

Edited by:

John Bergez
Start-to-Finish Core Content Series Editor, Pacifica, California

Gail Portnuff Venable, MS, CCC-SLP
Speech/Language Pathologist, San Francisco, California

Dorothy Tyack, MA
Learning Disabilities Specialist, San Francisco, California

Jerry Stemach, MS, CCC-SLP
Speech/Language Pathologist, Director of Content Development, Sonoma County, California

Graphics and Illustrations:

Photographs and illustrations are all created professionally and modified to provide the best possible support for the intended reader.
Front cover: © North Wind Picture Archives
Page 8: Courtesy of the Library of Congress, Prints and Photographs Division [LC-USZC4-5284]
Pages 14, 55: The Granger Collection, New York
Page 16: Courtesy of the Library of Congress, Prints and Photographs Division [LC-USZ62-10201]
Page 18: Courtesy of the Library of Congress, Prints and Photographs Division [LC-USZC4-1796]
Page 24: Courtesy of the Library of Congress, Prints and Photographs Division [LC-USZ62-100809]
Page 26: Courtesy of the Library of Congress, Prints and Photographs Division [LC-USZ62-103217]
Page 30: Courtesy of the Library of Congress, Prints and Photographs Division [LC-DIG-cwpb-01097]
Page 32: Courtesy of the Library of Congress, Prints and Photographs Division [LC-USZ62-52153]
Page 34: Courtesy of the Library of Congress, Prints and Photographs Division [LC-USZC4-1526]
Page 38: Courtesy of the Library of Congress, Prints and Photographs Division [LC-USZ62-51832]
Page 47: Courtesy of the Library of Congress, Prints and Photographs Division [LC-DIG-cwpb-00836]
Page 50: Courtesy of the Library of Congress, Prints and Photographs Division [LC-USZ62-2006]
Page 53: Courtesy of the Library of Congress, Prints and Photographs Division [LC-DIG-cwpb-05205]
Page 61 and back cover: Courtesy of the Library of Congress, Prints and Photographs Division [LC-USZC4-1754]
Page 62: Courtesy of the Library of Congress, Prints and Photographs Division [LC-USZ62-132939]
All other photos not credited here or with the photo are © Don Johnston Incorporated and its licensors.

Narration:

Professional actors and actresses read the text to build excitement and to model research-based elements of fluency: intonation, stress, prosody, phrase groupings and rate. The rate has been set to maximize comprehension for the reader.

Published by:

Don Johnston Incorporated
26799 West Commerce Drive
Volo, IL 60073

800.999.4660 USA Canada
800.889.5242 Technical Support
www.donjohnston.com

International Standard Book Number
ISBN 978-1-4105-0986-4

Contents

The American Civil War 4

Getting Started 6

Article 1
No Picnic:
The First Battle of Bull Run 10

Article 2
"Forever Free":
The Battle of Antietam 22

Article 3
"Brave Men, Living and Dead":
The Battle of Gettysburg 36

Article 4
Splitting the South:
The Siege of Vicksburg 52

Glossary 65

About the Author 66

About the Narrator 67

A Note to the Teacher 68

The American Civil War

The Civil War split the United States into two parts: the North, which was also called the **Union**, and the South, which was also called the **Confederate States**.

The war began when 11 Southern states tried to leave the United States and become a new country. These states thought that President Lincoln wanted to take away their right to own slaves. Lincoln fought to keep the United States together.

More than 600,000 Americans died in four years of fighting. In 1865, the North won the war and ended slavery in the United States.

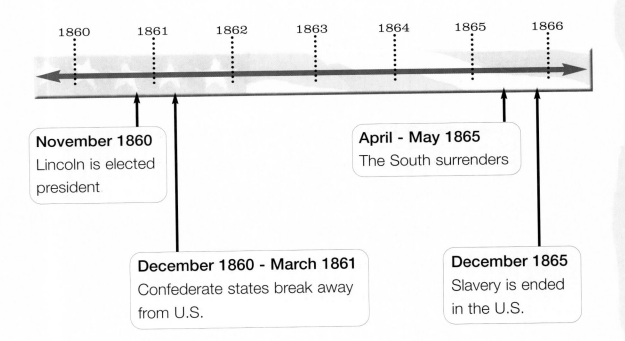

1860   1861   1862   1863   1864   1865   1866

November 1860
Lincoln is elected president

December 1860 - March 1861
Confederate states break away from U.S.

April - May 1865
The South surrenders

December 1865
Slavery is ended in the U.S.

Getting Started

Mary Chestnut kept a diary of her life during the Civil War. Mary lived in the Southern state of South Carolina.

At 4:30 in the morning on April 12, 1861, Mary was asleep in bed when a loud "boom" woke her up. A battle had started at Fort Sumter in Charleston, South Carolina. The battle was so close to Mary's house that she could hear the cannons.

Mary Chestnut

Fort Sumter was out in the water in Charleston harbor. The Union army was in control of the fort, but Charleston was in a Confederate state. The Confederates didn't want a Union fort in one of their states. When President Lincoln refused to give up the fort, the Confederates began bombing it with cannons. The "boom" that Mary heard was one of the first shots of the Civil War.

Confederates in Charleston bombed Fort Sumter with cannon fire.

The fight at Fort Sumter wasn't much of a battle. After a day and a half of bombing, the Union had to give up the fort. One Union soldier died during the fight. No one died on the Confederate side.

Mary Chestnut knew many people in the South who thought the rest of the Civil War would be just as easy as this battle. Most of them said that the war would be short. They didn't think many people would die. But they were wrong.

The Civil War wasn't quick or easy. It lasted four years, and it killed more than 600,000 Americans.

Nearly all the battles in the Civil War were much worse than the one at Fort Sumter. This book tells about four battles of the war. You'll learn why each battle was important. You'll also find out what it was like to fight in the Civil War.

Article 1

No Picnic: The First Battle of Bull Run

Questions this article will answer:

- **When the Civil War began, how long did people think it would last?**

- **How did Stonewall Jackson get his nickname?**

- **How did the First Battle of Bull Run change Northerners' ideas about the Civil War?**

Would you watch a war for fun? Would you bring a picnic to a battle?

That's just what some Northerners did in July 1861. It was three months after the fight at Fort Sumter. For the first time, big armies from the North and South came together in an important battle.

The battle took place near Bull Run Creek, about 25 miles (40 kilometers) from Washington, D.C. People from Washington packed picnic baskets and rode out to the battlefield in buggies that were pulled by horses. They thought it would be fun to see the Union soldiers beat the Confederates.

People from Washington packed picnic baskets and rode out to the battlefield in buggies.

The Northerners were wrong. It wasn't fun at all to watch hundreds of young men being killed that day. And when the fighting was over, Northerners knew that winning the war would be much harder than they had thought. In this article, you'll find out why they changed their minds.

The "Ninety Days' War"

When the Civil War began, most people thought it would be over quickly. President Lincoln called it "the Ninety Days' War." Lincoln asked Northern men to join the army for just 90 days.

Thousands of men signed up to fight for the Union. They were farmers, carpenters, and shopkeepers. Most of them did not know much about fighting. The Union general was Irvin McDowell. McDowell did not have enough time to train his new soldiers. People in the North wanted them to fight right away. The same thing was true in the South. Men rushed to join the Confederate army even though they were not trained soldiers.

Many Civil War soldiers were young farmers and shopkeepers who did not know much about fighting.

In July, McDowell and 35,000 Union men went out to fight about 23,000 Confederates near the town of Manassas, Virginia. People from Washington went out to watch the battle.

The two armies met at Bull Run Creek. Northerners called this fight the First Battle of Bull Run because there was a second battle in the same place later on. Southerners called it First Manassas.

When the battle began, many of the Northerners who were watching cheered because they thought the Union was winning. But as you will see, they were wrong.

"Like a Stone Wall"

The First Battle of Bull Run soon turned against the North. One reason was that the Confederates had a brave general named Thomas Jackson. Jackson became one of the war's first heroes.

General Thomas Jackson

General Jackson was in charge of a group of Confederate soldiers on a hill in the middle of the battlefield. Jackson kept his soldiers in their line, even when it seemed that the Union was winning the battle. No matter what happened, he did not let them move. Even when the Union army attacked them, they held their ground.

When the other Confederates saw what Jackson had done, they wanted to be as brave as he was. One general shouted, "Look at Jackson, standing there like a stone wall!" From then on, Thomas Jackson was called "Stonewall Jackson."

As the battle went on, more Confederate soldiers arrived. The Union started to lose. Most of the Union soldiers had promised to stay in the army for just 90 days. Some of them only had a few days left. They didn't want to die in the battle, so many of them ran away. The people from Washington left their picnics and ran for their lives.

Northerners found out that it was not fun to watch young men being killed at Bull Run.

Southern soldiers whooped and cheered. They had beaten the mighty Union!

Southerners were very proud of winning the battle. And they were proud of General Jackson. He had not run away. He had stood bravely, like a stone wall.

"Let Us Go to Work"

"We are whipped," a Northerner wrote after the First Battle of Bull Run. He meant that the North had lost badly. Northerners were ashamed that their soldiers had run away. People thought that General McDowell had done a bad job.

The battle showed Northerners that the war wouldn't be as easy as they had thought. But it also made them want to win more than ever. One man wrote a letter to a newspaper. In his letter, he said, "Let us go to work."

President Lincoln agreed. He asked for one million new soldiers, and he got them. This time, men signed up to fight for three years instead of 90 days. Lincoln also found a new general. His name was George McClellan. You will learn more about McClellan in Article 2.

President Abraham Lincoln

Many Southerners thought they
would win the war just because they had
won the Battle of Bull Run. This worried
Mary Chestnut. She wrote in her diary that
the Confederates were too sure of themselves.
She thought they still had a lot of fighting
to do.

Summary

In this article, you learned about the First Battle of Bull Run. Before this battle, many people in the North thought that the Civil War would be over in 90 days. Then the South won the battle, and Southerners found a hero — Stonewall Jackson. Northerners learned that they would need to work much harder to win the war.

Article 2

"Forever Free": The Battle of Antietam

Questions this article will answer:

- **Why did Robert E. Lee invade Maryland?**

- **Why was President Lincoln angry with George McClellan after the Battle of Antietam?**

- **What important announcement did Lincoln make after the Battle of Antietam?**

In the fall of 1862, things were not going well for the Union. It was more than a year after the First Battle of Bull Run, and the South seemed as strong as ever. In September, a Confederate army invaded the Northern state of Maryland. Before this time, most of the fighting had been in the South. Now the Confederates were boldly attacking the Union on its own land!

Then a Union soldier got very lucky. He found a piece of paper that had been dropped by a Confederate officer. It turned out to be the Confederate army's secret orders. The orders said that the Confederates were going to split up their army into three groups when they got to Maryland.

This news was a big help to the Union general, George McClellan.

If McClellan attacked right away, he could fight just one part of the Confederate army at a time. This would give him a better chance to win.

General George McClellan

But McClellan wanted to be very careful, and he took several days to make his own plans. This delay gave the Confederates time to get a lot of their army back together at Antietam Creek.

Antietam Creek was near the town of Sharpsburg, Maryland. There, the Union and Confederate armies met in one of the most terrible battles of the war. In this article, you will find out how the Battle of Antietam changed what the Civil War was about.

General Lee Attacks the North

The Confederate general at Antietam was Robert E. Lee. General Lee had taken a big risk by bringing his army into Maryland. His army was smaller than McClellan's army, and there was a chance it would be destroyed. If that happened, the South would probably lose the war.

General Robert E. Lee

But Lee had two important reasons for
invading the North. First, Lee believed that
people on the Union side might want to end
the war if the battles were fought on their
own land.

Lee's second reason for invading the North was this: he wanted to show countries like England that the Confederates were strong enough to stand up to the Union. He thought he could do this by winning some big battles in the North. If England and other countries in Europe believed that the South was strong, they might agree to treat the Confederate States as a new country — a country that was not part of the United States. And then it would be even harder for the Union to win the war.

In September 1862, Lee led his army out of Virginia. Lee and his men crossed the Potomac River and marched into Maryland. For the first time, the Confederates had invaded the North.

"Destroy Lee's Army!"

As you have read, General McClellan found out that Lee split up his army after crossing into Maryland. President Lincoln had already told McClellan to destroy Lee's army. Now McClellan had his chance. But he waited too long to attack, so Lee had time to get a lot of his army back together at Antietam Creek.

On the morning of September 17, McClellan finally attacked. "In a second the air was full of the hiss of bullets," one Union soldier said. Then the cannons opened fire. The cannonballs tore off soldiers' arms, legs, and heads.

The two armies fought until night came and darkness ended the bloody battle. In a single day, 23,000 soldiers were killed or wounded. It was the bloodiest day of the Civil War.

In the Battle of Antietam, 23,000 soldiers were killed or wounded in one day.

Lee's men fought well, but McClellan had many more soldiers than Lee did. Lee knew that he could not beat McClellan this time. He told his men to start marching back to Virginia.

McClellan could have chased after the Confederates, but he didn't. He let Lee and his men get away. This made President Lincoln very angry, and he fired McClellan a short time later.

A photo of dead soldiers at Antietam

A War for Freedom

It was not clear who had won the Battle of Antietam. (Southerners called it the Battle of Sharpsburg.) The number of killed and wounded men was about the same on both sides. But Lee had been forced to leave the North, and that was enough for President Lincoln to say the Union had won.

Lincoln had a special reason for saying that the Union had won the Battle of Antietam. He had decided to free all the slaves in the Confederate States. Lincoln believed that freeing the slaves would make the South weaker, because slaves did important work like growing food for Southern soldiers. But Lincoln wanted the North to win a big battle before he talked about setting the slaves free.

Winning a big battle would prove that the North was strong enough to make the South give up its slaves.

The North did well enough at Antietam for Lincoln to go ahead with his plans. Five days after the battle, Lincoln said that in January he would free all the slaves in states that were still fighting against the Union.

President Lincoln tells other leaders in the government about his plan to free the Southern slaves.

On January 1, 1863, Lincoln kept his promise in an announcement called the **Emancipation Proclamation**. Emancipation means setting people free. The words of the Proclamation said that the Southern slaves would be "forever free."

Lincoln's Proclamation gave many people a new reason to fight for the Union. Lincoln had always said that the Union was fighting to keep the United States together as one country. After the Emancipation Proclamation, many Northerners — and millions of African Americans — felt that the war was now about ending slavery. In this way, the Battle of Antietam helped to change the Civil War into a war for freedom.

President Lincoln's Emancipation Proclamation helped to change the Civil War into a war for freedom.

Summary

In this article, you learned how the Battle of Antietam changed the Civil War. In September 1862, General Robert E. Lee invaded the Northern state of Maryland.

General McClellan attacked Lee's army at Antietam Creek. After a terrible day of fighting, Lee had to give up, and he led his men back to the South.

President Lincoln said the North had won the battle, and he said that he planned to free all the slaves in the Confederate States. The announcement that freed the Southern slaves is called the Emancipation Proclamation. For many people, the Emancipation Proclamation meant that the war was now about ending slavery.

Article 3

"Brave Men, Living and Dead": The Battle of Gettysburg

Questions this article will answer:

- Why was General Lee surprised on the first day of the Battle of Gettysburg?

- Why did General George Pickett lead his soldiers right into the line of fire?

- Why was the Battle of Gettysburg so important?

In the spring of 1863, General Lee decided to invade the North again. By this time, many people in the North were tired of the war. Lee thought that if he could beat the Union army in a Northern state, the Northerners might decide to give up the fight. Lee also hoped that he would find food and supplies for his army in the North.

In June, Lee led 75,000 Confederate soldiers into the Northern state of Pennsylvania. A Union army of 90,000 men went to Pennsylvania to meet him.

General Lee led his army into Pennsylvania
to try to win the war for the South.

As Lee's men got close to the little town of Gettysburg, they heard about a building in the town that was full of shoes. A group of the men went to find the shoes, but instead of shoes, they found Union soldiers!

The Confederate and Union soldiers began shooting at each other. Both sides sent messengers on horseback to get help. Thousands of men from the two armies began hurrying toward Gettysburg. Soon the fight grew into the biggest battle of the Civil War. In this article, you will learn about this famous battle.

A Surprise at Gettysburg

When the shooting started at Gettysburg, General Lee was still miles away with the main part of his army. Lee was surprised to hear that a big fight had started. He had not known that the Union army was so close. Now, an important battle had started before Lee could get his army ready for it.

While Lee rushed toward the battlefield, the Confederates in Gettysburg pushed the Union soldiers out of the town. The Union soldiers climbed up a hill called Cemetery Hill. (*Cemetery* is another name for a graveyard.)

Look at the map on the next page. You can see Cemetery Hill and Culp's Hill below Gettysburg. Next came a **ridge** called Cemetery Ridge. (A ridge is a long strip of high ground.) There were two more hills at the southern end of Cemetery Ridge. These hills were called Little Round Top and Big Round Top.

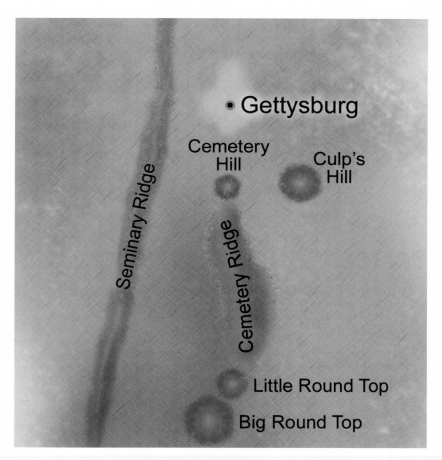

Gettysburg

Cemetery
Hill

Culp's
Hill

Seminary Ridge

Cemetery Ridge

Little Round Top

Big Round Top

The Union soldiers climbed up Cemetery Hill. The next morning, the Union line stretched almost all the way to Little Round Top.

At the end of the first day of fighting, the Union men were still on Cemetery Hill. Thousands more Union soldiers arrived during the night.

The next morning, the Union soldiers were lined up along the high ground from Culp's Hill and Cemetery Hill almost to Little Round Top. One Confederate general thought the Union line looked very strong. From the high ground, the Union men could fire down on any attackers. This general argued that the Confederates should leave Gettysburg and find a better place to fight the Union army.

General Lee refused. He pointed at Cemetery Hill and said, "The enemy is there, and I am going to attack him there."

All that day, General Lee kept trying to get his soldiers to the top of the hills on the two ends of Cemetery Ridge. None of his attacks worked. More than 18,000 men were killed or wounded in the terrible fighting.

On the second day of the battle, Lee's men attacked the hills on both ends of Cemetery Ridge.

Pickett's Charge

That night, Lee made up his mind to take a big risk. The next day, he would send General George Pickett to attack the middle of the Union line on Cemetery Ridge.

Lee's plan was risky, because Pickett's men would have to march right into the line of fire from the Union guns. But Lee believed that they could drive the Union soldiers off the ridge.

Lee began the attack the next morning. First, he fired his cannons at the Union line. Then General Pickett led more than 12,000 Confederates toward Cemetery Ridge. Row after row of Confederate soldiers marched toward the high ground and began climbing up the ridge. This attack is called Pickett's Charge.

At first, the Union guns were silent. But as Pickett's men came closer, the Northerners opened fire. Confederate soldiers screamed as the bullets and cannonballs tore into their bodies. While hundreds of men fell, others kept climbing toward the Union guns.

Some of the Confederates reached the top of the ridge. "Men fired into each other's faces, not five feet apart," one soldier remembered. "There were . . . men going down on their hands and knees, spinning around like tops . . . gulping blood." The Confederates nearly broke through, but the Union line held. The Southerners were forced back down the ridge.

Some of the Confederate soldiers reached the top of Cemetery Ridge.

Lee knew that the Battle of Gettysburg was over. The South had lost.

The next day, July 4, Lee led his army back toward Virginia. The army brought wagons carrying the dead bodies of Confederate soldiers. The line of wagons was 19 miles (30 kilometers) long.

The battle was terrible for both sides. In all, more than 50,000 Union and Confederate soldiers were dead, wounded, or missing after the three days of fighting at Gettysburg.

One of the thousands of Confederate soldiers who died at Gettysburg

Remembering Gettysburg

The Battle of Gettysburg was one of the most important battles of the Civil War for three reasons. The first reason is that after Gettysburg, Lee's army was never strong enough to invade the North again. The second reason is that winning at Gettysburg gave the Northerners hope, which helped them to keep fighting. Northerners were even more hopeful because the Union had another big win at the same time. It happened at a place called Vicksburg, in Mississippi. You will read about Vicksburg in the next article.

The third reason that the Battle of Gettysburg is important is that it led to a famous speech by President Lincoln. The speech is called the Gettysburg Address. (An "address" is another name for a speech.)

President Lincoln gave the speech in November, when the battlefield around Gettysburg became a cemetery for the Union soldiers who had died there.

In the speech, Lincoln said that Americans should always remember the men who had fought at Gettysburg. He called them "the brave men, living and dead." Lincoln said that the Union was fighting for the idea that people could govern themselves and stay together as one country. Lincoln called this idea "government of the people, by the people, and for the people." He said that this idea was worth fighting for, even though many men had lost their lives.

President Lincoln's speech at Gettysburg reminded Americans what Union soldiers were fighting — and dying — for.

Summary

In this article, you learned about the Battle of Gettysburg. In June 1863, General Robert E. Lee invaded Pennsylvania. Lee was surprised when a battle broke out at Gettysburg, but he decided to fight the Union army there anyway.

On the third day of the battle, Lee ordered General Pickett to lead a charge against the Union line on Cemetery Ridge. When the attack failed, Lee knew that the South had lost the battle.

The Battle of Gettysburg was important for three reasons. First, it was the last time that the South ever tried to invade the North. Second, winning the battle made the Northerners want to keep fighting. Third, the battle led to the Gettysburg Address, a famous speech by President Lincoln.

Article 4

Splitting the South: The Siege of Vicksburg

Questions this article will answer:

- **Why did General Grant want to capture Vicksburg?**

- **How did Grant get his army to Vicksburg?**

- **Why did the Confederates in Vicksburg give up?**

In May 1863, a Union army started to
attack Vicksburg, a town in the Southern
state of Mississippi. The army was led by
General Ulysses S. Grant.

General Ulysses S. Grant

Grant's attack on Vicksburg wasn't just
one battle that ended in a day, or even a week.
Instead, it was a **siege** that lasted six weeks.

53

In a siege, an army surrounds a town. The army does not let food or other supplies into the town. After a while, the soldiers and other people in the town run out of food, medicine, and other things they need. Then they have to give up or try to fight their way out.

General Grant's siege of Vicksburg led to a huge win for the North. In this article, you will find out why Grant wanted to capture Vicksburg, and you will learn how he did it.

Why Grant Wanted to Capture Vicksburg

General Grant thought that capturing Vicksburg would be a big step toward winning the war for the North. Why was Vicksburg so important? The first reason is that the town was built on a hill above the Mississippi River.

An army in Vicksburg could aim its guns at boats traveling on the river. In this way, that army could control who got to use the river. If the Union took charge of Vicksburg, it could stop the South from using the river to move soldiers or supplies.

Vicksburg was built on a hill above the Mississippi River.

Vicksburg was also important for another reason. There were Confederate states on both sides of the Mississippi. If the Union could get control of the river, the South would be split in two.

But capturing Vicksburg wasn't easy. In 1862, Union boats attacked the town from the river. These attacks failed. Then Grant tried attacking Vicksburg from the north, but his men could not get to the town. They were attacked by Confederate soldiers, and they also had a hard time getting through the swamps on the northern side of Vicksburg. (Swamps are places where the ground is very soft and wet.) Grant had to come up with a new plan.

A Risky March

In April 1863, Grant tried a new way of getting to Vicksburg. At this time, Grant's army was on the west side of the Mississippi River. Vicksburg was across the river, on the east side.

Grant knew that there was high, dry ground behind Vicksburg. Grant wanted to get his army across the river and all the way around Vicksburg so that he could attack the town from behind. The problem was how to get his army there.

Grant decided on a risky plan. First, he sent Union boats down the river past Vicksburg. Most of the boats got past Vicksburg safely. When the boats were about 30 miles south of Vicksburg, they stopped and waited for Grant.

Grant sent the Union boats down the river at night. Most of the boats made it past Vicksburg's guns without being sunk.

Next, Grant moved his army south until they met the Union boats. Then they used the boats to cross the river. Now Grant had his army on Vicksburg's side of the river. Then the army marched north and east until they were on the east side of Vicksburg. Now they could attack Vicksburg from the east.

You can see the path the army took in the map on this page.

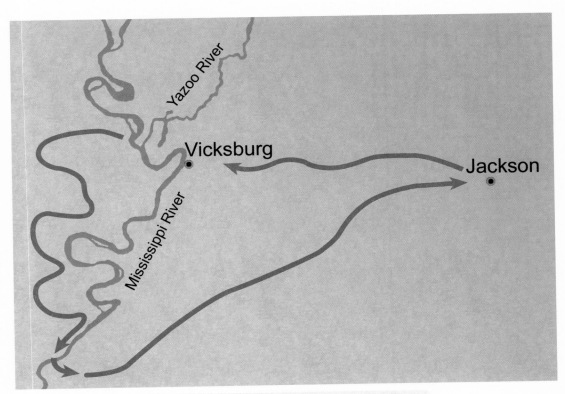

The red lines in this map show the path that Grant's army took to Vicksburg.

Grant was taking a big risk with this long march. After the Union soldiers crossed the river, they had to move through land that was controlled by the South.

The Union boats could not reach the soldiers with food and other supplies, so the men had to find what they needed in the countryside. Several times they also had to fight battles with Confederate soldiers who were trying to keep them away from Vicksburg.

Grant had taken a big chance, but his plan worked. By the middle of May, his army was camped outside of Vicksburg.

The Siege

When Grant got to Vicksburg, there were about 30,000 Confederate soldiers and 3000 townspeople in the town. Grant attacked right away, but the Confederates were able to fight him off. Grant decided that he would have to use a siege to capture the town.

For weeks, Grant's men did not let anyone out of Vicksburg. And they did not let any food or supplies *into* Vicksburg. Meanwhile, Union cannons bombed the town.

The siege of Vicksburg

Life in Vicksburg became a nightmare. The townspeople dug caves to hide from the cannon fire. As the soldiers and townspeople ran out of food, they had to eat dogs, cats, and even rats. After six weeks, there was almost nothing left to eat, and the Confederate commander had to give up.

The Confederate commander met with Grant to say that Vicksburg would surrender.

The Confederate soldiers marched out of Vicksburg on July 4 — the day that Americans call the birthday of the United States. On that same day, General Lee sadly led his soldiers away from Gettysburg. It was a great Fourth of July for the Union.

The siege of Vicksburg helped to make Grant a hero in the North. A short time later, Lincoln put Grant in charge of all the Union armies.

Grant knew that there was still a lot of hard fighting to do. But after Vicksburg and Gettysburg, he was sure that the Union would win the war.

Summary

In this article, you learned how General Ulysses S. Grant used a siege to capture the town of Vicksburg, Mississippi. Grant knew that if the Union soldiers could capture Vicksburg, the Union would have control of the Mississippi River. Then the South would be split in two.

Grant got his men to Vicksburg by leading them on a march through Southern land. Then he used a siege to make the Confederates give up the town. After the Union had won at Vicksburg and Gettysburg, Grant was sure that the North would win the Civil War.

Glossary

Word	Definition	Page
Confederate States	The Confederate States were the Southern states during the Civil War.	4
Emancipation Proclamation	the announcement by President Lincoln that freed the slaves in the **Confederate States**	33
ridge	a long strip of high ground	40
siege	In a siege, an army surrounds a city or town and doesn't let anyone in or out.	53
Union	The Union was the Northern states in the Civil War.	4

About the Author

Carrie Hall wrote her first poem when she was six years old. She called it "Fondue Party on My Head." Carrie didn't know what fondue was, but she liked the sound of the word. She has been writing ever since.

Carrie has written poems, newspaper articles, and short stories. In her free time, Carrie likes to read, paint pictures, spend time with her friends, and pet her two cats. But Carrie doesn't have much free time. She's always writing!

About the Narrator

John Sterchi has acted in movies, in plays, and in commercials. He has won awards for his acting and he was once in a movie with Tom Hanks! He has also narrated more than 300 books. John likes taking photos, fishing, watching basketball, and he's been to the Indy 500 18 times! John lives in Chicago with his two turtles, George and Lennie.

A Note to the Teacher

Start-to-Finish Core Content books are designed to help students achieve success in reading to learn. From the provocative cover question to the carefully structured and considerate text, these books promote inquiry, active engagement, and understanding. Not only do students learn curriculum-relevant content, but they learn how to read with understanding. Here are some of the features that make these books such powerful aids in teaching and learning.

Structure That Supports Inquiry and Understanding

Core Content books are carefully structured to encourage students to ask questions, identify main ideas, and understand how ideas relate to one another. The structural features of the Gold Core Content books include the following:

- **"Getting Started":** A concise introduction engages students in the book's topic and explicitly states what they will learn.
- **Clearly focused articles:** Each of the following articles focuses on a single topic at a length that makes for a comfortable session of reading.
- **"Questions This Article Will Answer":** Provocative questions following the article title reflect the article's main ideas. Each question corresponds to a heading within the article.
- **Article introduction:** An engaging opening leads to a clear statement of the article topic.
- **Carefully worded headings:** The headings within each article are carefully worded to signal the main idea of the section and reflect the opening questions.
- **Clear topic statements:** Within each article section, the main idea is explicitly stated so that students can distinguish it from supporting details.
- **"Summary":** A brief Summary in each article recaptures the main ideas signaled by the opening questions, text headings, and topic statements.

Text That Is Written for Success™

Every page of a Core Content book is the product of a skilled team of educators, writers, and editors who understand your students' needs. The text features of these books include the following:

- **Mature treatment of grade level curriculum:** Core Content is age and grade-appropriate for the older student who is actively acquiring reading skills. The books also contain information that may be new to any student in the class, empowering Core Content readers to contribute interesting information to class discussions.
- **Idioms and vocabulary:** The text limits the density of new vocabulary and carefully introduces new words, new meanings of familiar words, and idioms. New subject-specific terms are bold-faced and included in the Glossary.
- **Background knowledge:** The text assumes little prior knowledge and anchors the reader using familiar examples and analogies.
- **Sentence structure:** The text uses simple sentence structures whenever possible, but where complex sentences are needed to clarify links between ideas, the structures used are those which research has shown to enhance comprehension.

For More Information

To find out more about Start-to-Finish Core Content, visit www.donjohnston.com for full product information, standards and research base.